# DESTINATION *Australia*

## MAGNIFICENT PANORAMIC VIEWS

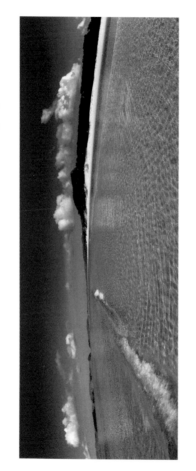

PANOGRAPHS®
PUBLISHING PTY LTD

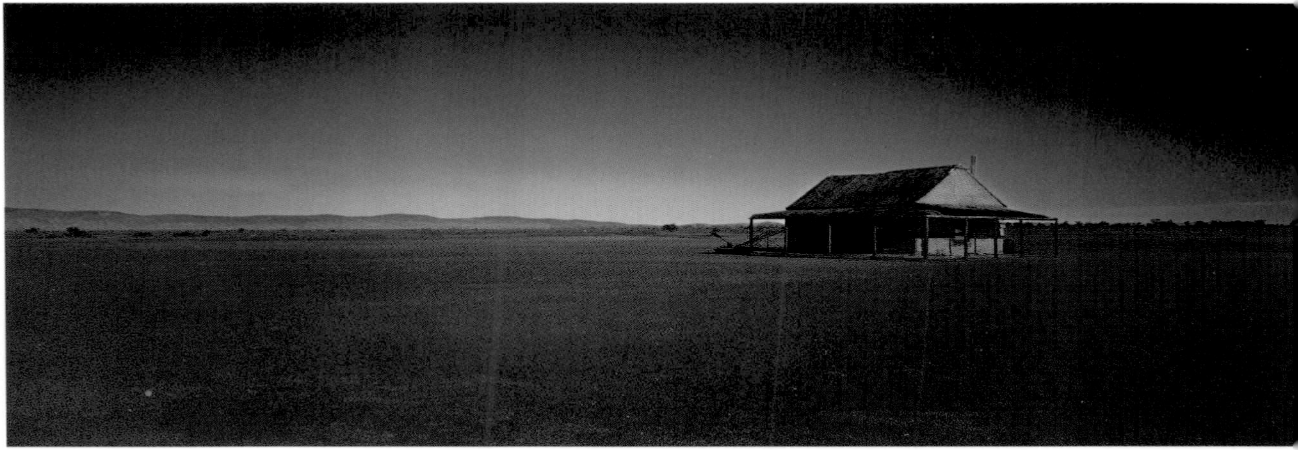

**V**ast in proportion and wonderful in its diversity, Australia is a continent loved by visitors from all over the world. In area, it is a country as large as Europe, measuring more than 7,700,000 square kilometres. But with a population of just twenty million - the majority living in a few cities along its eastern fringe - Australia still boasts huge tracts of virtually untouched land and sea. Much of the best is preserved in over five hundred national parks, including such magnificent World Heritage listed areas as the Great Barrier Reef and Kakadu.

The diversity of landscapes is breathtaking. Australia's 36,000 kilometre coastline includes hundreds of sparkling beaches as well as the spectacular weather-worn cliffs of the continent's south. Inland there are vast areas of desert and scrub, and deeply-eroded mountain ranges containing some of the world's oldest rocks. To the north there are important pockets of ancient rainforest, and along the Great Dividing Range there are large forests of Australia's famous eucalypts.

Captured here by renowned panoramic landscape photographer, Ken Duncan, Australia's natural wonders glow with vibrant colour and light and are beautifully complemented by a range of inspirational quotes. From the famous rockforms of the desert to the sweeping high country of the Great Divide, Destination Australia is a wonderful snapshot of an unforgettable continent.

PERSIUS

*He conquers who endures.*

TITLE PAGE
*Whitehaven Beach, Qld*

PREVIOUS PAGE
*Aganst All Odds, Silverton, NSW*

THIS PAGE
*On the Road to Gundagai, NSW*

*Until you spread
your wings,
you'll have no idea
how far you can fly.*

ANON

More than 2000 islands and nearly 3000
interconnected coral reefs dot Queensland's
magnificent Great Barrier Reef. Here at Whitsunday
Island, the spectacular swirled waters of Hill Inlet
glow like an aqua-coloured jewel.

**THIS PAGE**
Whitsunday Island, Qld

**NEXT PAGE**
Heart of a Nation, Uluru, NT

KEN DUNCAN

*Life is about
what we give
not about
what we get.*

Though relatively small (about the size of Switzerland),
Tasmania boasts a wide variety of landscapes - from
glacial mountains to thick forests and rolling hills.
At Russell Falls, a veil-like curtain of water flows
through dense temperate rainforest.

*Russell Falls, Tas*

*A will finds a way.*

ORISON SWETT MARDEN

Western Australia is frontier country, a vast and barely
populated expanse with an abundance of unique
natural features. Seen here soaked in the morning sun,
Mitchell Falls is one of the great monuments of the
state's Kimberley Plateau.

**THIS PAGE**
*Dawn of Creation, Mitchell Falls, WA*

**NEXT PAGE**
*Early miner's cottage, Hillend, NSW*

*All of our dreams
can come true
if we have the courage
to pursue them.*

Stretching four hundred kilometres into the outback,
the Flinders Ranges are one of South Australia's
greatest natural features. The rocks are ancient and
magnificently rugged, worn by millennia of slow and
ceaseless weathering.

*Arkaba Woolshed, Flinders Ranges, SA*

17

I was taught
that the way of progress
is neither
swift nor easy.

MARIE CURIE

THIS PAGE
Maguk Falls, Kakadu, NT

NEXT PAGE
Paradise, Fantome Island, Qld

MAHATMA GANDHI

*There is more to life than increasing its speed.*

Piccaninny Creek,
Purnululu National Park, WA

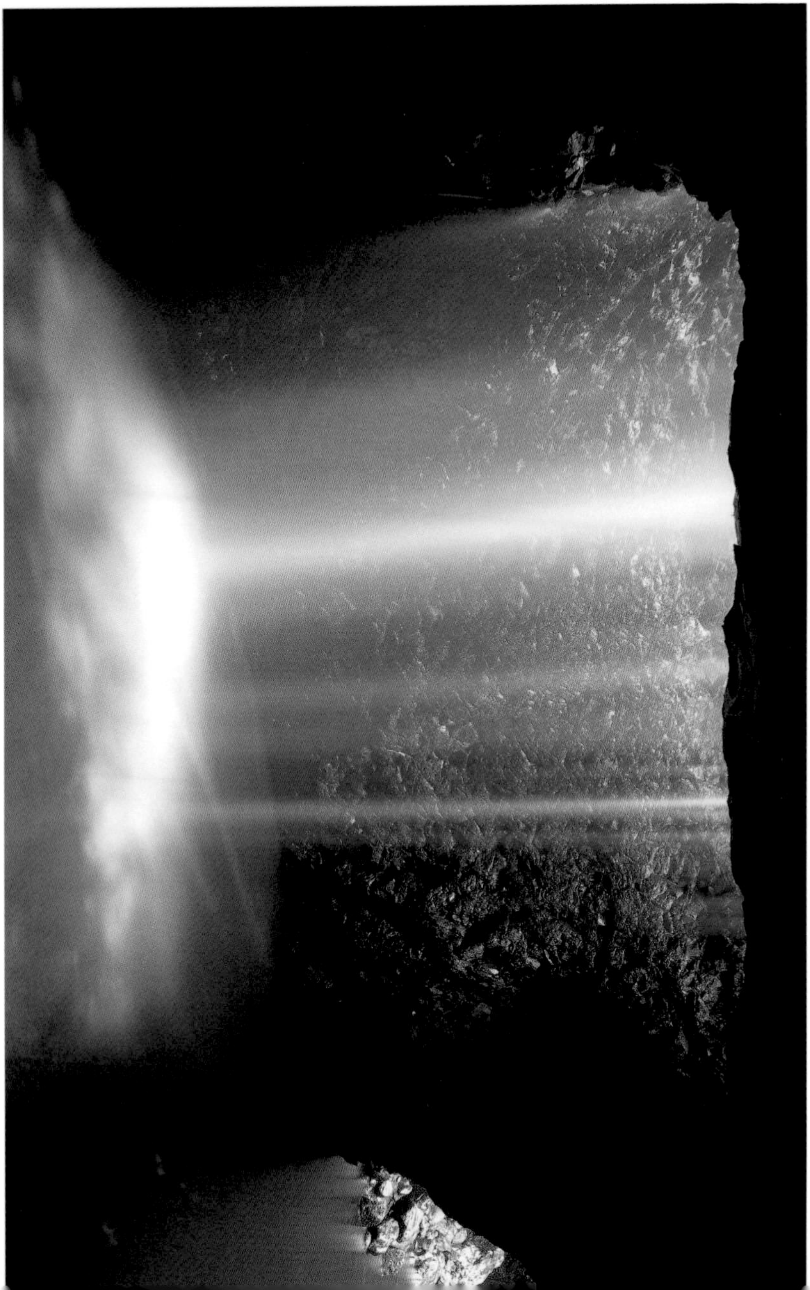

MAHATMA GANDHI

*Where there is love*
*there is life.*

THIS PAGE
*Natural Arch, Qld*

NEXT PAGE
*Southern Dreaming, The Twelve Apostles, Vic*

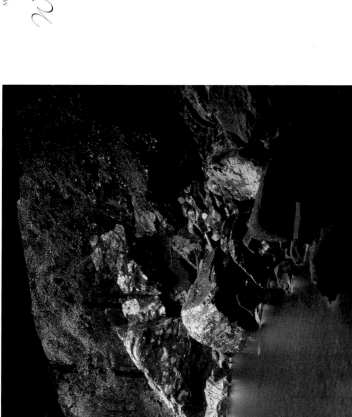

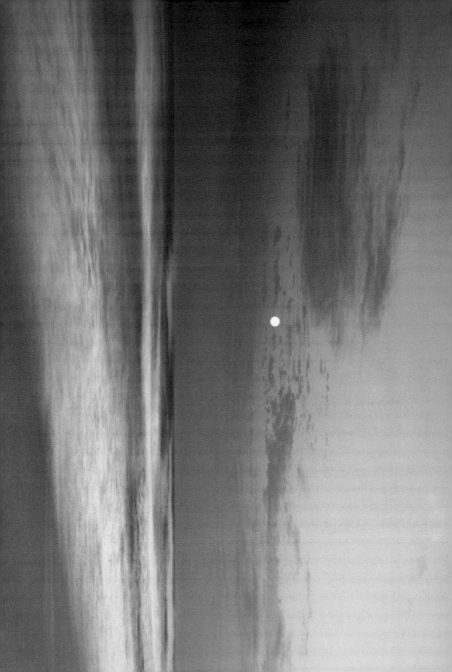

ALBERT EINSTEIN

*The most beautiful thing*
*we can experience*
*is the mysterious.*

PREVIOUS PAGE
Misty morning, Strzelecki Ranges, Vic

THIS PAGE
The Labyrinth, Tas

WILLIAM JENNINGS BRYAN

*Destiny is not
a matter of chance,
it is a matter of choice.*

Magnificently poised on a hilltop in the Alpine National Park, this slab hut built for the film The Man from Snowy River shows off some of Victoria's renowned high country - just one of many landscapes in Australia's smallest mainland state.

THIS PAGE
Broad Horizons, Craig's Hut, Vic

NEXT PAGE
Forgotten Dreams, Burra, SA

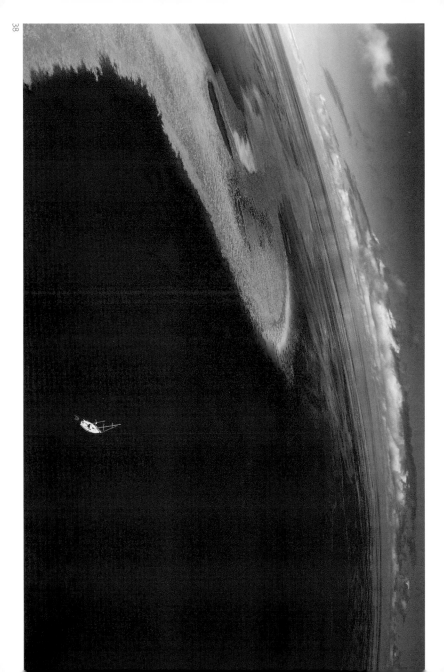

CHRISTOPHER COLUMBUS

*Following the light*
*of the sun,*
*we left the Old World.*

PREVIOUS PAGE
*Hopetoun Falls, Vic*

THIS PAGE
*Sailing Away, Great Barrier Reef, Qld*

NAPOLEON I

*Courage is like love;*
*it must have hope*
*for nourishment.*

Western New South Wales is characterised by vast red plains, but in the east the slopes of the Great Divide are famous for their magnificent swathes of eucalypt forest. Here at Ebor Falls, water and mist are delightfully framed by the forest canopy.

**THIS PAGE**
Peace in the Valley, Ebor Falls, NSW

**NEXT PAGE**
The Three Sisters, NSW

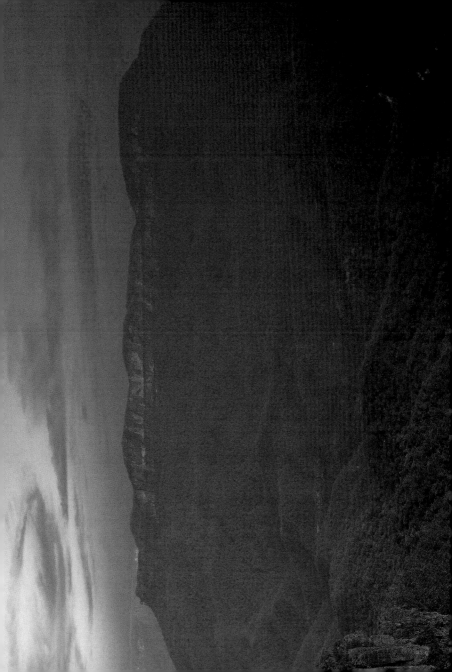

*Deeds, not stones, are the true monuments of the great.*

JOHN L MOTLEY

The remarkable domed rocks of Kata Tjuta
(which means "many heads") are the most famous
natural feature in the Northern Territory after Uluru.
This sunset view captures one group of domes in a
spectacular deep red glow.

PREVIOUS PAGE
Kitchen Hut, Cradle Mountain, Tas

THIS PAGE
Sunset, Kata Tjuta, NT

*The Pinnacles, WA*

DESTINATION AUSTRALIA
First published 2005
Revised edition printed 2007
by Panographs® Publishing Pty Ltd
ABN 21 050 235 606
PO Box 3015, Wamberal,
NSW, 2260, Australia
Telephone +61 2 4367 6777
Email: panos@kenduncan.com

The National Library of Australia
Cataloguing-in-Publication entry:
Duncan, Ken
Destination Australia:
magnificent panoramic views.
Rev. ed.
ISBN 9780977573011.
1. Australia - Pictorial works. I. Title
919.400222

To view the range of Ken Duncan's
panoramic Limited Edition Prints
visit our Galleries:

- **Shop T232 Erina Fair, Erina, NSW**
  **Telephone +61 2 4367 6701**
- **73 George Street, The Rocks,**
  **Sydney, NSW**
  **Telephone +61 2 9241 3460**
- **Shop U6 Southgate,**
  **Melbourne, Vic**
  **Telephone +61 3 9686 8022**
- **Shop 14 Hunter Valley**
  **Gardens Village,**
  **Broke Road, Pokolbin, NSW**
  **Telephone +61 2 4998 6711**

VISIT THE KEN DUNCAN GALLERY ONLINE: www.kenduncan.com